Because

I HAVE FOUND IN JESUS CHRIST THE ANSWER
TO MY EVERY NEED, AND BECAUSE I AM
EAGER TO SHARE THE BLESSINGS OF MY FAITH
WITH OTHERS

I am happy to present this book to

_____

with the prayer

THAT THE READING OF ITS PAGES WILL LEAD
TO A DEEPER UNDERSTANDING OF THE GLORIES
OF THE CHRISTIAN FAITH AND TO A FIRMER
CONFIDENCE IN JESUS CHRIST, OUR SAVIOR

_____

SIGNED

What Jesus Means to Me

What
JESUS
Means to Me

By H. W. GOCKEL

CPH.
SAINT LOUIS

9 780570 030218

Manufactured in the U. S. A.

32 33 34 35 36 37 38 39   03 02 01 00 99 98

Preface

JESUS means more than the world to me. The last name to occupy my conscious thoughts at night — the first name to enter my waking mind each morning — is the name "all other names above," the eternal name of Jesus.

But why? — What is it about the name of Jesus that bridges every day and night, that bridges every night and day, and goes with me wherever I might be? What is it in the name of Jesus that makes it the golden sunset of every evening, the bright and cheering dawn of every morning? Am I perhaps the victim of some sweet delusion?

By no means! Jesus is a fact. He is a tremendous fact. He is an eternal ever-present fact. He is the one sure fact around which everything in heaven and earth revolves. He

was a fact "in the beginning," before the
heavens and the earth were made.

And He is still the world's most powerful
fact today — always present in the lives of
those who believe in Him, always helping,
always guiding; for He has promised: "Lo,
I am with you alway, even unto the end of the
world."

Jesus is many things to me. He is Pardon,
Peace, Joy, Hope, Assurance, Contentment,
and Life Everlasting. He is my Friend, my
Companion, my Counselor, my Prophet, my
Priest, and my King. And He can be all of
that for *you*. Indeed, He *wants* to be all of
that for you. "Behold, I stand at the door
and knock," He says; "if any man hear My
voice and open the door, I will come in to him
and will sup with him, and he with Me."

The experiences and convictions which are
recorded in this little volume are by no means
to be regarded as the experiences and convictions only of the author. They are the glorious
convictions of millions of Christian men and
women throughout the world today: men and

women in your town, in your neighborhood, perhaps on your own street.

They were the convictions of millions upon millions who lived and died during the long ages past. They were the deep and abiding convictions, for instance, of Horatius Bonar, who lived one hundred years ago and who summed up all his religious experience in the well-known lines:

> *I heard the voice of Jesus say:*
> *"Come unto Me and rest;*
> *Lay down, thou weary one, lay down*
> *Thy head upon My breast."*
> *I came to Jesus as I was,*
> *Weary and worn and sad;*
> *I found in Him a resting place,*
> *And He has made me glad.*

Jesus can make *you* glad! What He has meant to hundreds of millions down through the centuries, and what He still means to uncounted multitudes today, He can mean to *you*. In order that you, too, might find in Him "a resting place," this book, by the provi-

dence of God, has come into your hands. If
you have not learned to know Jesus Christ as
the Son of God — your Savior, your Master,
and your Friend — nothing is more important
for you right now than that you read these
pages.   H. W. G.

Contents

Life

FOR me to live is Christ!"

If you were to ask me what Jesus means to me, I could think of no better reply than these six short words of the Apostle Paul, written nineteen hundred years ago.

The artist who spends the late and early hours in the company of his paint and brush and canvas may very well say: "For me to live is *art*." The musician who thinks and dreams and speaks of nothing but his music may very well say: "For me to live is *music*." In a similar but in an unspeakably higher sense I can truly say: "For me to live is *Christ*."

In Christ I have found the final answer to my greatest needs, the abiding satisfaction of my deepest longings, the complete dispelling of my darkest fears, and the rich fulfillment of my highest aspirations. — Is it any wonder that I say: "For me to live is *Christ*"?

There is not a blessing in my life which, if I trace it back to the hand that gave it, does not lead me back to the Son of God. No matter where I turn, no matter where I look — if there is anything good, anything true, anything that has brought lasting joy and gladness into my life — I recognize it ultimately as a gift which has come to me through faith in Jesus Christ, my Savior.

In Him, above all, I have found complete forgiveness for all my sins. The Bible tells me: "He loved me and gave Himself for me." It assures me: "The blood of Jesus Christ, God's Son, cleanseth us from all sin." And it promises, without qualification: "Whosoever believeth in Him should not perish, but have everlasting life." Because I believe these promises and have been assured by God Himself that they are true, I can spend every hour of the day in the full assurance that I am prepared to meet my God. My sins have been forgiven through faith in Jesus Christ, my Lord.

This knowledge has filled my heart with a peace and joy and hope which mere human words can never utter. The poet despaired of

ever finding words to describe the thrill of
a life which had found its peace with God
through faith in Christ, when he penned the
words:

> *The love of Jesus, what it is,*
> *None but His loved ones know.*

I have that peace. I am assured of that love.
Through Christ I have been born into a life
of assurance and joy and hope. Through
Christ I have been made a child of God
and an heir of heaven.

That is why I can say with the Apostle
Paul and with all Christians of all ages:
"Christ is my life."

> *As the branch is to the vine,*
> *I am His, and He is mine.*

I am bound to Him by a debt of gratitude
that all eternity could not pay. And He is
bound to me by a love so limitless that no
measurement could ever plumb its depths.

It is this close and intimate relationship with
Jesus Christ, the Son of God, which is the
source of my inner strength and joy. In this

close relationship with Him I have found the only answer to the deepest cravings of my soul: pardon, peace, power, provision, companionship, hope, truth, assurance, joy, and heaven.

And having found these, I have found *life* — life, full and free; life, glorious and triumphant; the "abundant life," which God has guaranteed to those who come to Him through Jesus Christ, His Son. I have experienced what millions of other believers have learned, namely, that "if any man be in Christ, he is a new creature; old things are passed away; behold, all things are become new."

Among the old things that have passed out of my life are sin, and guilt, and fear; uncertainty, and doubt, and dark despair. And among the new things that have entered my life are assurance of God's love, assurance of His guidance and protection, companionship with Christ, and the certain prospect of eternal life with Him in heaven. "Old things are passed away," indeed; "all things are become new."

These are the glories of the Christian life, the life that is "hid with Christ in God." And these are the glories which we shall take up, one by one, in each of the succeeding chapters of this book.

Only he who can say with the Apostle Paul, "For me to live is Christ," can complete the sentence as Paul first spoke it — "and to die is gain."

> *O Jesus, King most wonderful,*
> *Thou Conqueror renowned,*
> *Thou Sweetness most ineffable,*
> *In whom all joys are found.*
>
> *O Jesus, Light of all below,*
> *Thou Fount of life and fire!*
> *Surpassing all the joys we know,*
> *All that we can desire —*
>
> *May every heart confess Thy name*
> *And ever Thee adore*
> *And, seeking Thee, itself inflame*
> *To seek Thee more and more.*

Pardon

O_F all the things that Jesus means to me He is, above all else, my Savior. By His suffering and death *in my place* upon the cross He has paid the penalty of all my sins. The Bible assures me that though my "sins be as scarlet, they shall be as white as snow; though they be red like crimson, they shall be as wool." And why? Because "the blood of Jesus Christ, God's Son, cleanseth us from all sin."

I know that to many people today the word "sin" does not mean very much. Sin, they say, is a mistake or a fault which can't be helped and which therefore is not so serious. Sin to many people is just a flaw which somehow or other will be forgotten when God begins to settle His accounts. There are men and women who shrug off the idea of sin as being — "just one of those things."

But God thinks otherwise. No matter how lightly men may speak of sin, no matter how cleverly they may seek to explain it or excuse it, God has placed His curse upon it. "The soul that sinneth, it shall die." "The wages of sin is death." "Cursed is everyone that continueth not in all things which are written in the Book of the Law to do them."

Sin, according to God, is a frightful thing which, if it remains unforgiven, will result in the eternal separation of a man from his Maker.

I know, too, that some people associate the idea of sin only with criminals: with murderers, adulterers, and public scoundrels. But God says: "There is no difference, for *all* have sinned." "They are *all* gone aside; they are altogether become filthy; there is none that doeth good; no, not one!" "There is not a just man upon earth that doeth good and sinneth not." "We are all as an unclean thing, and all our righteousnesses are as filthy rags." "Whosoever shall keep the whole Law and yet offend in one point, he is guilty of all." Those are God's words.

In His sight there is no difference, as far as the fact of sin is concerned, between the cultured white-haired matron, the respectable family man, the loving mother, the refined librarian, and the man who was sentenced last week to die for murder. There may be a difference in degree. But there is no difference in the fact. For "the Scripture hath concluded all under sin." "There is no difference."

According to God's reckoning, sin is every departure from His holy will in thoughts or words or deeds. To have an impure thought, to say an unkind word, to be disrespectful, envious, or quarrelsome, is just as surely a sin as are robbery, theft, or wicked violence. Jesus told the people of His day that hatred and anger were an infraction of God's commandments: "Thou shalt not kill." If that is true, and Jesus says it is, then who can count the sins of which every one of us is guilty every day of his life!

There are people to whom this consciousness of sin has never become very real. While they are ready, in a general way, to admit their shortcomings and regret them, they have never been crushed or terrified by the dread-

ful implications of their sin. The great Apostle
Paul, when he became conscious of the terrific
burden of his guilt, cried out: "Oh, wretched
man that I am! Who shall deliver me from
the body of this death?" The piercing pain
of sin had cut deep into his anguished soul.

David, the man after God's own heart, when
he came to realize that his sins were great
enough to separate him from the presence
of God into all eternity, exclaimed: "When
I kept silence, my bones waxed old through
my roaring all the day long. For day and
night Thy hand was heavy upon me. My
moisture is turned into the drought of summer." David had learned the terrible reality
of his sin and the still more frightful reality
of sin's consequences. Sin, *his* sin, had become
real to him — frightfully real!

I, too, have felt the dreadful weight of sin.
Again and again I have had to say with the
Apostle Paul: "I know that in me (that is, in
my flesh) dwelleth no good thing." With
David I have had to confess: "Behold, I was
shapen in iniquity, and in sin did my mother

conceive me." As I look back to my childhood days, I see the undeniable truth of God's verdict: "The imagination of man's heart is evil from his youth." I must agree with Him when He says that by nature I was among "the children of wrath, even as others."

But why speak about my sin — when I began to speak about my Savior! Because no man can tell what Jesus means to him until he has first told what *sin* has meant to him. To tell the full story of a rescue at sea, one must first tell the story of the shipwreck which made that rescue necessary. No man is ready to accept Christ as his Savior from hell and damnation until he has felt the hot breath of hell blow over his quivering conscience. If Christ is to be our Savior, we must know from what we must be saved.

Right here is where Jesus stepped into my life and filled it with a joy and a peace which surpass all understanding. For in Him I have God's assurance of full and free forgiveness of the entire burden of my sin. Without Christ there would have been, there could have been, no forgiveness. Without Christ the course of my life would have led straight to a judgment which would have been too terrible to contemplate. For "none of them can by any means redeem his brother nor give to God a ransom for him; for the redemption of their soul is precious, and it ceaseth forever." "Neither is there salvation in any other; for there is none other name under heaven given among men whereby we must be saved." No other name than the blessed name of Jesus!

The Bible tells us: "When the fullness of the time was come, God sent forth His Son, made of a woman, made under the Law, to redeem them that were under the Law, that we might receive the adoption of sons." Christ, the eternal Son of God, came down from heaven to accomplish what I was unable to do — and He did it in my place, as my Substitute.

I was unable to keep God's Law. So Christ kept it for me. The commandments that I have broken *He has kept* — and His record has been written to my account. That is the wonderful assurance that God has given me in the fourth and fifth chapters of Paul's Epistle to the Romans. What I could not do, Christ did for me. And now, to use the word of Scripture, God has "imputed" Christ's righteousness to my account. He has written *His* record to *my* credit! Paul says: "Not having my own righteousness . . . but that which is . . . of God by faith."

> *Jesus, Thy blood and righteousness*
> *My beauty are, my glorious dress,*
> *Wherein before my God I'll stand*
> *When I shall reach the heavenly land.*

But more! Christ also suffered the punishment of all my sins. He assumed the guilt which was mine. He paid the penalty which I should have paid. He took my place before the bar of God's justice and by His payment of my debt secured my freedom. Because of Christ's atonement I have been acquitted. This atonement theme is the golden thread of assurance which God has woven throughout the pages of the Bible.

Already seven hundred years before Jesus was born, the Prophet Isaiah looked forward to the Savior's death on Calvary and wrote: "Surely *He* hath borne *our* griefs and carried *our* sorrows. . . . *He* was wounded for *our* transgressions, *He* was bruised for *our* iniquities; the chastisement of *our* peace was upon *Him;* and with *His* stripes *we* are healed. All we like sheep have gone astray; we have turned everyone to his own way; and the Lord hath laid on *Him* the iniquity of *us* all."

Jesus Himself, speaking of the purpose of His coming into the world, said that He had come to "give His life a ransom for many." In the night in which He was betrayed He gave each of His disciples a piece of bread with the words: "This is My body, which is broken for you." And He gave them the cup with the words: "This is My blood of the New Testament, which is shed for many for the remission of sins." His death in the place of sinners was to purchase forgiveness for all mankind.

Late one night, speaking to a leader of the Jews, Jesus revealed the purpose of His coming into the world and particularly the purpose of His suffering and death. He said to Nicodemus: "As Moses lifted up the serpent in the wilderness, even so must the Son of Man be lifted up [on the cross], that whosoever believeth in Him should not perish, but have eternal life. For God so loved the world that He gave His only-begotten Son, that whosoever believeth in Him should not perish, but have everlasting life."

This was the glorious fact that the Apostles proclaimed throughout the world soon after Christ's ascension into heaven. "Christ died for our sins!" "We were reconciled to God by the death of His Son." "The blood of Jesus Christ, His Son, cleanseth us from all sin." "Who His own self bare [bore] our sins in His own body on the tree [the cross]." "He loved me and gave Himself for me." "Christ hath redeemed us from the curse of the Law, being made a curse for us." "Ye were redeemed . . . by the precious blood of Christ."

"If any man sin, we have an Advocate with the Father — Jesus Christ, the Righteous. And He is the Propitiation [the Reconciliation] for our sins; and not for ours only, but also for the sins of the whole world." These are all direct quotations from the Bible, written by men who had been commissioned by Christ to spread His saving Gospel.

In view of these clear Bible statements, what does Jesus mean to me? Above all else, He means forgiveness! His life, His suffering, His death were all for me. Through faith in Him I have come to share in the unspeakable assurance of those of whom the Apostle says: "There is therefore now no condemnation to them which are in Christ Jesus." No guilt! No fear! No condemnation! For all my sins have been washed away in the atoning blood of Christ.

It was after the Apostle Paul had contemplated the marvelous love of God in Christ that he burst forth with the jubilant hymn of faith: "What shall we say to these things? If God be for us, who can be against us? He that spared not His own Son, but delivered Him up for us all, how shall He not with Him also freely give us all things? Who shall lay anything to the charge of God's elect? It is God that justifieth. Who is He that condemneth? It is Christ that died, yea rather, that is risen again, who is even at the right hand of God, who also maketh intercession for us. Who shall separate us from the love of Christ? Shall tribulation, or distress, or persecution, or famine, or nakedness, or peril, or sword? . . . Nay, in all these things we are more than conquerors through Him that loved us. For I am persuaded that neither death, nor life, nor angels, nor principalities, nor powers, nor things present, nor things to come, nor height, nor depth, nor any other creature shall be able to separate us from the love of God, which is in Christ Jesus, our Lord."

That is the supreme assurance of every man who comes to God through Christ. And that is *my* assurance. Through Christ I have a loving God in heaven. Through Christ the wall

of partition between His Father and me has
been broken down forever. Through Christ
I have free access to the Father-heart of
God — because through Christ my sins are all
forgiven. That is why I can join with the
millions who confess:

> *Not what these hands have done*
> *Can save this guilty soul;*
> *Not what this toiling flesh has borne*
> *Can make my spirit whole.*

> *Not what I feel or do*
> *Can give me peace with God;*
> *Not all my prayers and sighs and tears*
> *Can bear the awful load.*

> *Thy work alone, O Christ,*
> *Can ease this weight of sin;*
> *Thy blood alone, O Lamb of God,*
> *Can give me peace within.*

> *Thy love to me, O God,*
> *Not mine, O Lord, to Thee,*
> *Can rid me of this dark unrest*
> *And set my spirit free.*

Thy grace alone, O God,
To me can pardon speak;
Thy power alone, O Son of God,
Can this sore bondage break.

I bless the Christ of God;
I rest on Love Divine;
And with unfaltering lip and heart
I call this Savior mine!

What does Jesus mean to me? He means many things. But, above all else, He means — *pardon!*

Peace

Two artists vied with each other to see which could produce a painting which would depict the idea of peace. One painted the picture of a quiet lake away up on a mountaintop. Not a breeze was stirring. Not a bird was flying. Not a ripple disturbed the quiet waters. All was perfect silence. That, in the opinion of the first artist, was the truest picture of peace.

The second artist painted a picture of a roaring waterfall, with a mighty tree hanging over it. In the crotch of a limb bending over the turbulent waters and almost within reach of the rising spray — he painted a tiny sparrow sitting calm and unperturbed upon her little nest. In the midst of the mighty roar, surrounded by what seemed to be frightful danger, the sparrow hadn't a worry in the world: her cozy little nest was snug in the crotch of a mighty oak — on a branch which the waters could not reach.

Both artists agreed that the second picture came closer to depicting the highest conception of peace. Perhaps neither of them knew that in the second picture they had found an excellent portrayal of the peace which a Christian believer has found in his Savior.

The true peace and rest of the Christian life is not a peace and rest which is to be found somewhere in a distant world of make-believe, but a peace and rest which is to be found right here in the very midst of a world of trial and trouble.

It was the night before His enemies nailed Him to a cross that Jesus said to His disciples — and to His followers of all time — *"Peace* I leave with you, My *peace* I give unto you; not as the world giveth, give I unto you. Let not your heart be troubled, neither let it be afraid. . . . These things I have spoken unto you that in Me ye might have *peace.* In the world ye shall have tribulation; but be of good cheer; I have overcome the world."

In the world — tribulation; in Christ — peace. This is the experience of every believer, as it has been the experience of the children of God in all ages. There need be no denying the fact, this world is not a congenial place for the practice of the Christian life. I am not speaking of the world of joy and beauty which God has given us — the verdant meadows, the enchanting hillsides, the majestic mountain peaks, the blue canopy of heaven, and the soft and downy clouds which float like angel pillows across a summer's sky. No, all of this is lovely beyond description.

But I am thinking of the world in the sense in which the Bible often speaks of it — the human family as it exists apart from God. It is of that world that the Bible says: "Love not the world, neither the things that are in the world . . . the lust of the flesh and the lust of the eyes and the pride of life. . . ." That is the world of ugliness, of sordidness, of meanness, with which we find ourselves surrounded day in and day out — the world whose path is strewn with broken hearts and blasted lives and whose graves are watered with the tears of deep and dark despair.

In our passage through *that* world, says
Jesus, we shall have tribulation. But — "in
Me, peace!" That has been my great dis-
covery. In Christ I have found peace in the
midst of all adversity, peace in the midst of
conflict, peace in the face of opposition, peace
beneath the weight of every burden. The
Apostle Paul, toward the end of a life which
had been beset by unnumbered difficulties,
wrote to his friends: "Christ is our Peace!"
What did he mean?

Above all, he meant that in Christ he had
found peace with God. Paul had been a great
sinner. He had persecuted the church of
Christ. But by the grace of God he had come
to a shocking realization of his enormous
guilt. "Oh, wretched man that I am!" he exclaimed. He became conscious of a "wall of
partition" which, if it would not be removed,
would forever separate him from the presence
of his God.

But — and this was the greatest revelation
of his life — that wall had been removed! In
spite of his sins he and his heavenly Father

were on good terms. Christ had brought
about a complete reconciliation. That is why
Paul could write to the Romans: "Therefore,
being justified by faith, we have *peace* with
God through our Lord Jesus Christ." That is
why he could end his letter to them with the
familiar greeting: "Now, the God of hope fill
you with all joy and *peace* in believing." And
that is why he could speak the familiar benediction upon his fellow Christians: "The *peace*
of God, which passeth all understanding, shall
keep your hearts and minds through Christ
Jesus."

That peace of God is mine, and it is mine
through Christ Jesus. It is rooted forever in
the knowledge that through Christ God and
I are completely reconciled. We are "at one"
through the at-one-ment of the Savior. Let
my conscience accuse me, let the world point
its mocking finger at the record of my failures,
let Satan and hell seek to throw fear into my
soul by reminding me of the depths of my
iniquity — I say, let the devil, the world, and
my flesh try to rob me of the inner peace

which I have found in Christ's forgiveness —
they shall never undermine my heart's assurance:

Now I have found the firm foundation
  Which holds mine anchor ever sure;
'Twas laid before the world's creation
  In Christ my Savior's wounds secure;
Foundation which unmoved shall stay
When heaven and earth will pass away.

Though earthly trials should oppress me
  And cares from day to day increase;
Though this vain world should sore
    distress me
  And seek to rob my Savior's peace;
Though I be brought down to the dust,
Still in His mercy I will trust.

Sure, His great love shall make me willing
  To bear my lot and not to fret.
While He my restless heart is stilling,
  May I His mercy not forget!
No matter what may be the test,
His love shall be my only rest.

That is the foundation, the cornerstone, on which my inner quiet rests. I am at *peace with God*. And being at peace with God, I am at peace with myself. I have received an inner strength which prepares me for all of life's vicissitudes.

I am at peace in the midst of conflict. What if things are going wrong? What if, because of my loyalty to Christ, the winds of opposition blow stiff and strong? What if the waters of life are ruffled by the fierce storms of enmity and persecution? Let the storms rage. I am at peace with God! We are told that no matter how furious the storm on the surface of the ocean, no matter how high the billows roll and how deep the watery valleys that stand between them — the deepest caverns of the ocean know nothing about the storms that rage above. Down there in the ocean depths all is calm, all is quiet. So, too, is the heart that has found its peace with God through Christ. No storm can disturb its inner quiet.

And I am at peace beneath the weight of every burden. It would be foolish and untrue to say that the Christian life does not have its trials. The gnawing pang of loneliness, the heavy hand of sickness, the bitter pain of disappointment, the icy finger of inevitable death — all of these fall to the lot of the Christian as they do to every man. But there is a difference, a great difference! Through Christ the believer knows he is at peace with God; and being at peace with his Maker, he knows that even sorrow and sickness and death are part of God's *gracious* plan for him. And so he rests in quiet peace beneath the weight of every burden.

Above all, I shall dwell in peace when I am called upon to make that fateful journey through the valley of death. With Simeon of old I shall be able to welcome "Death's bright angel" with the hymn of triumph: "Lord, now lettest Thou Thy servant depart *in peace,* according to Thy word, for mine eyes have seen Thy Salvation." With the sweet singer of Israel I shall be able to say: "Yea, though

I walk through the valley of the shadow of death, I will fear no evil, for Thou art with me." And whence shall I draw this courage? From the love of Christ, through whose life and death I am at peace with God.

The Bible tells us: "Thou wilt keep him in perfect peace whose mind is stayed on Thee." Millions of believers will testify that they have found more positive psychology in those few words than in a whole library of technical volumes on the subject. Millions of Christians, having learned to know the love of God in Christ, have learned to throw their entire weight on God, trusting that "underneath are the everlasting arms." Into His hands they commit all of their *yesterdays* — knowing that in His mercy He will forgive them. Into His hands they commit *today* — knowing that it is another day of grace. And into His hands they commit all of their *tomorrows* — knowing that all of His mercies which have been "new unto us every morning" will be just as new, just as sure, and just as all-sufficing tomorrow

as they are today. Theirs is the peace of a life
that is "hid with Christ in God."

That is why I say Jesus is my Peace.

In the Cross of Christ I glory,
Towering o'er the wrecks of time;
All the light of sacred story
Gathers round its head sublime.

When the woes of life o'ertake me,
Hopes deceive, and fears annoy,
Never shall the Cross forsake me;
Lo, it glows with peace and joy.

When the sun of bliss is beaming
Light and love upon my way,
From the Cross the radiance streaming
Adds more luster to the day.

Bane and blessing, pain and pleasure,
By the Cross are sanctified;
Peace is there that knows no measure,
Joys that through all time abide.

Power

A MOTHER visited her boy at college. Upon entering his room, her eye swept across the walls, which were covered with more than a dozen suggestive pictures. Her heart was grieved, but she said nothing.

Several days later the mailman delivered a package to the young man. It was a gift from his mother — a beautifully framed picture of the head of Christ.

Proudly the boy hung the picture on the wall above his desk. That night, before he went to bed, he removed the pin-up picture which hung closest to the face of Christ. The next day another picture was consigned to the wastebasket. Day after day the pictures began to disappear from the walls until only one remained — the picture of the Savior.

No one had lectured to the boy, no one had told him to remove the other pictures. The power of the contemplation of Christ had made it impossible for him to keep the other pictures on his walls.

Christ *is* like that! His is the power of heaven. Once a man has found his salvation in the blood of Jesus Christ, he will find the power of Christ *expelling* the evil from his heart and *impelling* him to deeds of Christian love and virtue. The power to fight sin and the power to do right are gifts which Christ bestows on all believers.

But we must belong to Christ before we can lay claim to that power. He says: "As the branch cannot bear fruit of itself except it abide in the vine, no more can ye except ye abide in Me. I am the *Vine,* ye are the branches. He that abideth in Me, and I in him, the same bringeth forth much fruit; for without Me ye can do nothing." Only he who clings to Christ by a living faith will have the power to resist sin, to overcome temptation, and to lead a life of Christian goodness. Outside of the Vine — severed from the only Source of spiritual life — there is no spiritual power. "Without Me ye can do nothing."

The Apostle Paul, who was transformed from a spiritual weakling into one of the world's spiritual giants, made no secret of the source of his power. "I can do all things through Christ, which strengtheneth me," he says. And in another place he writes: "I live; yet not I, *but Christ liveth in me;* and the life which I now live in the flesh I live by the faith of the Son of God, who loved me and gave Himself for me."

Where did Paul get the power to stop in his tracks, to put an end to his worthless career, to lead a life of charity and decency, to stand up under the ridicule and opposition of his countrymen, to endure beating and stoning and bitter persecution, to sing hymns of praise in prison, and finally to give his life in payment for his faith? Where did he find this power to endure and to achieve? "I can do all things through Christ, which strengtheneth me," he says. "Nevertheless I live; yet not I, but Christ liveth in me." Surely, if anyone had asked Paul what Jesus meant to him, he would have answered: "Among the many

other things that Jesus means to me, He
means *power*—power to overcome evil, power
to endure, power to gain a continuing victory."

I, too, have found Christ to be my inex-
haustible Source of spiritual and moral power.
In moments of temptation, in the hour of trial,
in days of doubt and darkness, I have fled to
"Jesus, Lover of my soul," with the prayer:

> *Reach me out Thy gracious hand,*
> *While I of Thy strength receive!*

And without fail I have received His strength:
strength to stand in the midst of the tempest,
strength to outlast the storm, strength to bear
the burden of the cross, strength to resist the
onslaught of sin — or, having fallen, to tread
the path of the prodigal back to the Father's
house and to be assured of full and free forgiveness. These victories were by no means
mine. Left to myself, to my own puny powers
of resistance or endurance, I would have suc-
cumbed long since. "Not that we are sufficient
of ourselves . . . but our sufficiency is of God."
"By the grace of God I am what I am." These

confessions of the penitent Apostle are also mine.

To receive power from Christ I must, of course, believe in Him. I must see in Him the eternal Son of God, my Savior, my ever-present Friend. Paul was a man. He is dead. He cannot help me. Peter, James, and John were men. They are dead. They cannot help me. But Christ is the eternal Son of God, the almighty Creator and Sustainer of the universe. By His resurrection from the dead He has proved Himself to be the Father's only Son, who lives and reigns with Him in highest heaven. "He was declared to be the Son of God *with power* . . . by the resurrection from the dead," says Paul. And at another place the Scriptures say of Him: "He upholds all things by the word of His power." With Him all things are possible, for He Himself has said: "All power is given unto Me in heaven and in earth." And now in that power I am privileged to share.

But how do I make application for my share of that power? How is this strength

poured into my weakness? How do I make
contact? I receive power from Christ by believing. I accept the helping hand of Christ
by simply trusting Him. He has promised
me pardon for my sin, peace for my soul,
strength in the hour of trouble, courage in
the face of difficulty, power in the moment of
temptation — and I receive this pardon, peace,
and power simply by trusting that He will
keep His promise.

> *I am trusting Thee, Lord Jesus,*
> *Trusting only Thee;*
> *Trusting Thee for full salvation,*
> *Great and free.*

> *I am trusting Thee for power;*
> *Thine can never fail.*
> *Words which Thou Thyself shalt give me*
> *Must prevail.*

I seek daily reassurance of His power
through prayer. More than once when the
burden seemed too heavy, when the assign-
ment seemed too great, when my shoulders

seemed too weak to bear the burden, I have called upon Him; and always either He has lightened the burden to match my strength, or He has increased my strength to match the burden. And in His power, I have prevailed.

Perhaps the best illustration of the power of Christ resting upon those who believe in Him is given us in the lives of His disciples. If ever there was a band of defeated, dejected, and frightened men, it was the little group of eleven whose world collapsed when their Master died. Like frightened sheep, they were huddled in a back room on a side street in the city of Jerusalem — weak, timid, quaking, afraid of their own shadows!

But what a difference when once they had been assured of their Lord's resurrection from the dead! He lives! He lives! He is not dead! He is with us, as He promised! The knowledge that their dearest Friend was alive again transformed a lonely, empty world into a world that was charged with the power of

His presence. No matter where they went from that time on, they knew that the omnipresent Christ was with them. No combination of hell or world could successfully withstand them. They had become conscious of a tremendous power hitherto unknown to them: the power of the helping Christ.

And so they went forth to live courageous and victorious lives. Peter, the weakling who had deserted his Lord in His moment of utmost need, all of a sudden becomes a bold preacher of the Word. Stephen stands like a pillar and is unafraid. John preaches boldly in the Temple. And Saul of Tarsus sets out to turn the world upside down for Christ. "Ye shall receive power," Christ had told them. Now they had received that power.

And down through the centuries the pages of history are filled with the names of men and women who have overcome the world in the power of Christ. Millions upon millions have confessed Christ to be the Source of their spiritual power and have come to Christ

again and again with the humble prayer of
Charles Wesley:

> *Jesus, my Truth, my Way,*
> *My sure, unerring Light,*
> *On Thee my feeble soul I stay,*
> *Which Thou wilt lead aright.*
>
> *Thou seest my feebleness;*
> *Jesus, be Thou my Pow'r,*
> *My Help and Refuge in distress,*
> *My Fortress and my Tow'r.*
>
> *Give me to trust in Thee;*
> *Be Thou my sure Abode;*
> *My Horn and Rock and Buckler be,*
> *My Savior and my God.*
>
> *Myself I cannot save,*
> *Myself I cannot keep;*
> *But strength in Thee I surely have,*
> *Whose eyelids never sleep.*
>
> *My soul to Thee alone*
> *Now, therefore, I commend.*
> *Thou, Jesus, having loved Thine own,*
> *Wilt love me to the end.*

What does Jesus mean to me? What did
He mean to the faithful few whom He sent
out to preach His Gospel? What did He mean
to the millions who have lived and died in
devotion to His name? Among many other
things, He has meant *power* — power to resist
sin; power to lead the fuller, happier life;
power to bear the burdens of each day; power
to achieve the final victory. "As many as
received Him, to them gave He *power to
become the sons of God,* even to them that
believe on His name."

Provision

THE story is told of a man who invited a few friends to a most unusual dinner. As the guests entered the dining room, they noticed a silver screen at one end of the spacious room and a picture projector at the other. Before the oysters were served, the light went out, and there upon the screen they saw men toiling in the sea and among the rocks, in the cold mist, dredging for the oysters they were to eat.

When the vegetables came, they saw the picture of little children who should have been in school or at play, but instead were shelling peas in a distant canning factory. When the bread was brought in, they were shown pictures of plowing and harrowing and sowing and reaping and threshing and grinding — the infinite labor and pains which were necessary before that bread could come to them. The meat was served, and they beheld the hard life of the men on the plains and in the stockyards and on the railroads, all of which was necessary before those dainty and delicious portions of meat could be theirs.

When they had finished, they knew, as they had never known before, the sacrifice of toil and time on the part of others which lies behind the common things in life. Unfortunately, the demonstration, as good as it was, was not complete. For had the host thought just one step farther, he would have finished his visual demonstration with a picture of the Savior with hands raised in blessing, and on the screen he would have thrown the well-known verse of Scripture:

> *"The eyes of all wait upon Thee,*
> *O Lord, and Thou givest them their*
> *meat in due season. Thou openest*
> *Thine hand and satisfiest the desire*
> *of every living thing."*

For it is Jesus, the Christ, the omnipotent Son of God, who provides all mankind with daily food. Speaking of Jesus, the Bible says:

"All things were made by Him; and without Him was not anything made that was made." St. Paul writes to the Ephesians, praising the almighty God, "who created all things by Jesus Christ." And to the Colossians the same Apostle extols the almighty power of Christ, "who is the Image of the invisible God, the First-born of every creature; for by Him were all things created that are in heaven and that are in earth." In other words, Jesus Christ, together with the Father and the Holy Spirit, is the Creator of the universe. And not only the Creator, but also the Sustainer, for the Bible says of Him: "He upholds all things by the word of His power."

I have found in Jesus Christ my great Provider, who cares for all my needs, both temporal and spiritual. Writing about God's great providence, Martin Luther included the following lines in the Small Catechism, which he wrote for the children of his day, more than four hundred years ago:

"I believe that God has made me and all creatures; that He has given me my body and

soul, eyes, ears, and all my members, my
reason and all my senses, and still preserves
them; also clothing and shoes, meat and
drink, house and home, wife and children,
fields, cattle, and all my goods; that He richly
and daily provides me with all that I need to
support this body and life; that He defends
me against all danger and guards and pro-
tects me from all evil; and all this purely out
of fatherly, divine goodness and mercy, without any merit or worthiness in me, for all
which it is my duty to thank and praise, to
serve and obey Him. This is most certainly
true."

Yes, this is most certainly true. But it is
true only because God has become my Father
through Jesus Christ. "Ye are all the children
of God by faith in Christ Jesus," the Bible
tells us. I am assured of God's love and
providence only because Jesus, by His suffering and death, has restored me to sonship
with the Father. It is true, in a certain sense,
the unbelieving children of the world receive
the same temporal blessings which God be-

stows upon His children. "He maketh His sun to rise on the evil and on the good, and sendeth rain on the just and on the unjust." But their relationship to God is not that of Father and child; theirs is not the loving confidence which a loving son has toward his father; theirs is merely the helpless dependence of a creature upon his Creator. And that makes all the difference in the world!

A Roman emperor, after a brilliant military campaign, was returning in triumph to Rome. Kings and princes were chained to his chariot wheels as trophies of his triumph. Cheering crowds filled the city streets to pay homage to the conquering hero. As the spectacular procession passed through the city's center thoroughfare, a little girl, wild with joy, dashed toward the moving chariot. The strong arm of a uniformed guard stopped her. "That is the chariot of the emperor," he said. "You must not try to touch it." The little one replied: "He may be your emperor, but he is *my father!*" A moment later she was not only in the chariot, but clasped fondly in her father's arms. Even so it is with those who have come to God through Christ. While God is the Emperor of all men, He is that and infinitely more to those who accept His Son as Savior; He is their Father!

And as their Father, He is moved by love to provide for all of their necessities. It is true, His Father-love may find it necessary to withhold some physical blessings from His children. But the hand that withholds is attached to the heart that loves, and that is all we need to know. One of the most beautiful passages of the Bible is that section of the Sermon on the Mount where Jesus speaks movingly to His disciples about the tender care of His Father for all His children. "Take no thought for your life," He says, "what ye shall eat or what ye shall drink, nor yet for your body, what ye shall put on. Is not the life more than meat, and the body more than raiment? Behold the fowls of the air; for they sow not, neither do they reap, nor gather into barns; yet your heavenly Father feedeth

them. Are ye not much better than they? . . .
Consider the lilies of the field, how they
grow; they toil not, neither do they spin. And
yet I say unto you that even Solomon in all
his glory was not arrayed like one of these.
Wherefore, if God so clothe the grass of the
field, which today is and tomorrow is cast
into the oven, shall He not much more clothe
you, O ye of little faith? Therefore take no
thought, saying, What shall we eat? or, What
shall we drink? or, Wherewithal shall we be
clothed? . . . Your heavenly Father knoweth
that ye have need of all these things. But
seek ye first the kingdom of God and His
righteousness; and all these things shall be
added unto you."

"Your Father!" What a tender, reassuring
touch these words give to the promise of the
Savior! "Your heavenly Father knoweth that
ye have need of all these things." The weary
child at the end of day will often confide his
wants and needs to his earthly father and then
drift off to peaceful slumber. It is enough
that Father knows! His love will find a way.

His love will contrive the means to satisfy tomorrow's needs.

Our heavenly Father does know our every want and wish. And He is abundantly able and willing to provide. "He that spared not His own Son, but delivered Him up for us all, how shall He not with Him also freely give us all things?" There is no need in our life, however great or small, that God does not know and which He will not fill if it be necessary for our temporal and eternal happiness. "My God shall supply *all* your needs according to His riches in glory by Christ Jesus," says Paul.

But will He? Can I trust Him? Can I be sure that each succeeding day will find a sufficient measure of His grace and goodness to see me and my loved ones through? Yes, I can be sure. John, in His Gospel, speaks of the heavenly glory of Jesus and says: "Of His fullness have all we received — and grace for grace." Literally, "grace *upon* grace." Christ's goodness pours in upon us as the waves of the sea. As the one comes, there is always another close behind, and then another and another. Christ's capacity and willingness to provide are unlimited and eternal.

A well-to-do man died and left instructions to his wife to give a certain portion of his wealth to a poor minister who had frequently remembered the family with deeds of kindness. The widow thought it would be best to turn the money over to the minister in regular installments; so she mailed him $25.00, and inside the envelope she placed a little slip of paper upon which was written: "More to follow." Every two weeks, without fail, the elderly man would find a package of money in his post box with the identical message: "More to follow."

"More to follow!" That is Christ's unbreakable pledge to all who believe in Him. The blessings which we receive today are but a pledge of those which we shall receive tomorrow; and those we receive tomorrow will bear the pledge of heaven: "More to follow."

His mercies are new every morning. His compassions fail not.

The Psalmist writes: "I have been young and now am old; yet have I not seen the righteous forsaken, nor his seed begging bread." He who could feed five thousand people with "five barley loaves and two small fishes" is still capable of supporting those who trust in Him. His multiplying hand has never lost its power. Jesus says: "I am the Good Shepherd." The believer says: "The Lord is my Shepherd, I shall not want." He daily supplies me with rich provision. I need not fear for tomorrow's needs, for He has promised to supply them. The Bible assures the believer: "Godliness is profitable unto all things, having promise of *the life that now is* and of that which is to come." Christ has promised to take care also of the bodily needs of those who come to God by Him.

I have found Christ to be my heavenly Provider. Since I have accepted Him as Savior and Sovereign of my life, I have entrusted

Him also with the provision of my physical
necessities. I have endeavored, with the help
of God, to live up to the Scriptural pattern:
"casting all your care upon Him, for He
careth for you." And I have found Him
supremely able and willing to provide.

> *Savior, I follow on,*
> *Guided by Thee,*
> *Seeing not yet the hand*
> *That leadeth me.*
> *Hushed be my heart and still,*
> *Fear I no further ill,*
> *Only to meet Thy will*
> *My will shall be.*
>
> *Riven the rock for me*
> *Thirst to relieve,*
> *Manna from heaven falls*
> *Fresh ev'ry eve.*
> *Never a want severe*
> *Causeth my eye a tear*
> *But Thou dost whisper near,*
> *"Only believe."*

Savior, I long to walk
   Closer with Thee;
Led by Thy guiding hand,
   Ever to be
Constantly near Thy side,
Quickened and purified,
Living for Him who died
   Freely for me.

Companionship

There come moments into the life of every one of us when the world seems to pass us by — and we are forced to eat the bread of loneliness. The rich and the poor, the mighty and the weak, the dweller in the palace and the tenant in the shack — all have felt at some time or another the piercing pang which comes with the knowledge of being unnoticed, unneeded, or unwanted.

Perhaps no pain is more poignant than the sharp and sudden realization that our friends have found us to be "expendable," that, while the march of life is passing by our door, we have been left to sit alone. The human heart cries out against the aching pain of loneliness. And its cries can never be completely silenced until it has found the solace and the strength which come from true companionship.

I have found that true Companion — in Christ!

Scarcely an hour passes without my being

clearly conscious of His presence. Morning,
noon, and night I know that He is with me.
Again and again I find myself in earnest con-
versation, sharing with Him my problems and
perplexities, seeking guidance and direction.
In the midst of a busy day I find myself
telling Him about my joys, sharing with Him
my triumphs, and speaking to Him in tones
of gratitude for blessings without number.
And in each case the very assurance of His
presence and His interest in my joys and sorrows pours new life, new courage, and new
gladness into my soul.

But can I be sure that He is there? Can
I be sure that He is with me and that He can
hear the flood of thoughts which I have never
uttered? Yes, I *can* be sure. This intimate
companionship between the Savior and the
individual believer is one of the most beautiful assurances of the Bible. While He was
still on earth Jesus spoke fondly and frequently about this close companionship which
was to exist between Him and every man
who would put his trust in Him.

During the closing days of His life this fellowship seemed to be uppermost in all His thinking. Again and again He assured His followers that even after His death (yes, *especially* after His death and resurrection and ascension into heaven) He would be united with them in the closest fellowship the world has ever known. "My sheep hear My voice," He said, "and I know them, and they follow Me. And I give unto them eternal life; and they shall never perish; neither shall any man pluck them out of My hand."

A little later He assured His followers: "At that day ye shall know that I am in My Father, and ye in Me, and *I in you.*" And again: "I am the Vine, ye are the branches. He that abideth in Me, and *I in him,* the same bringeth forth much fruit." Not many hours before His crucifixion He prayed to His heavenly Father, pleading for those who believed in Him: ". . . that they may be one, even as We are One: *I in them,* and Thou in Me. . . ." And finally, just before He ascended visibly

into heaven, He gave the climax assurance
to all Christians of all times: "Lo, I am with
you alway, even unto the end of the world."
Christ is the Heaven-sent Companion to every
heart that puts its trust in Him.

It is comforting beyond measure to see
how the Bible abounds in assurances of God's
presence in the lives of individual believers.
"I will never leave thee nor forsake thee."
"My presence shall go with thee." "Fear thou
not, for I am with thee; be not dismayed, for
I am thy God. I will strengthen thee; yea,
I will help thee; yea, I will uphold thee with
the right hand of My righteousness." "I will
be with thee: I will not fail thee, nor forsake
thee. Be strong and of good courage." The
companionship of the individual believer with
his God and Savior is a companionship based
upon the faithful pledges of an eternal Friend.

> *Jesus, Thou art mine forever,*
> *Dearer far than earth to me;*
> *Neither life nor death shall sever*
> *Those sweet ties which bind to Thee.*

*All were drear to me and lonely
   If Thy presence gladdened not;
While I sing to Thee, Thee only,
   Mine's an ever blissful lot.*

*Jesus, Thou art mine forever,
   Suffer not my feet to stray;
Let me in my weakness never
   Cast my priceless pearl away.*

I was brought into this intimate companionship with Christ through the covenant of Baptism. "For as many of you as have been baptized into Christ have put on Christ." This intimate fellowship with Christ is strengthened by my frequent presence at His Supper. There in an unspeakably sublime manner He draws near to me and assures me of His loving presence, His abundant pardon, and His mighty power. "Take, eat, this is My body. . . . Drink ye all of it, this is My blood." "This do in remembrance of Me." I attend His Holy Supper frequently for the strengthening of my faith, for the reassurance

of my fellowship with Him, and for renewed
power to lead an ever better Christian life.

But in Christ I have also found a larger
fellowship. I have been united in the bonds
of spiritual companionship with millions of
fellow Christians, both those now living and
those who long since have gone to join the
Savior. "For we, being many, are one bread
and one body; for we are all partakers of that
one bread," says Paul. The name of Jesus
unites more people than does any other name.
I have a sense of kinship, a sense of fellowship, not only with the Prophets and Apostles,
not only with martyrs and the saints of all
ages, but with scores and hundreds of thousands of likeminded people in my own de-
nomination, and with uncounted millions of
believers in every quarter of the globe. For,
"we, being many, are one body in Christ, and
everyone members one of another," says the
Apostle. That is why Paul, writing to the
handful of Christians in the city of Ephesus,
could say: "Now, therefore, ye are no more
strangers and foreigners, but fellow citizens

with the saints and of the household of God."
They were no longer alone; they had been
accepted into the family of God, and their
brethren and sisters in the faith were more
numerous than they had ever dreamed.

I, too, have been accepted into the family
of God through faith in Jesus Christ. I, too,
share in the comfort and strength which comes
from the knowledge that millions of my fellow
men are my brethren and sisters in Christ
and that we who believe in Christ are the
children of one Father. It was this blessed
assurance which inspired John Fawcett to
write the lines of the beautiful hynm:

> *Blest be the tie that binds*
> *Our hearts in Christian love;*
> *The fellowship of kindred minds*
> *Is like to that above.*

> *Before our Father's throne*
> *We pour our ardent prayers;*
> *Our fears, our hopes, our aims, are one,*
> *Our comforts and our cares.*

From sorrow, toil, and pain,
  And sin we shall be free
And perfect love and friendship reign
  Through all eternity.

Through Christ I am walking through the world hand in hand with the greatest, the highest, and the noblest names of history. What illustrious company! Through Christ I am walking through the world hand in hand with those people who are doing the best, the finest, and the loveliest things in the world today. What glorious companionship! Through Christ I have become a part of that family to which the world owes everything that it has received from two thousand years of Christian influence. What splendid fellowship! Through Christ I have joined hands with those people of whom the Savior says: "Ye are the salt of the earth. . . . Ye are the light of the world." What a sublime association!

Alone? Lonely? Yes, sometimes it may seem so. But I am never really alone. In

Christ I have a true Companion, a Friend that never fails. And through faith in His redemption I have become a "fellow citizen with the saints" and a member of the "household of God." Who could ask for better company?

And so, if you ask me: "What does Jesus mean to you?" I answer: "Jesus means many things to me. One of them is *companionship,* true and constant — *fellowship,* intimate and sure."

Hope

A missionary to South Africa tells an interesting story. In the course of his travels he was called upon to make a long journey with Cecil Rhodes, perhaps the most influential of the British leaders in that country. The missionary was struck by the depression and gloom which seemed to surround this otherwise great man. One day he gathered sufficient courage to put the point-blank question: "Mr. Rhodes, are you a happy man?"

"I shall never forget," the missionary goes on to report, "how he threw himself back against the cushions and, gripping the arm of the seat, exclaimed, while looking at me in a tense attitude: 'Happy? I — happy? No, indeed!' After a while I said to him: 'Mr. Rhodes, there is only one place where we can find real happiness, and that is down at the feet of the crucified Savior, because only there can we be freed from our sins.'

After some time Mr. Rhodes said to me slowly and emphatically: 'I would give all that I possess if I could believe what you believe!' "

Mr. Rhodes had money, friends, power, fame, and whatever else this world may offer any person. He lived in a lovely home and was highly respected by thousands. But he had not found happiness, because he had not found hope. He had not been assured of a future which would bring him those things which his heart lacked most — peace, joy, assurance, the confident prospect of eternal bliss and glory.

Those things are to be found only in Christ. Nowhere else in this whole wide world can men find any foundation on which to build their hopes. They have tried it, but always they have failed. During the prosperous years following the First World War, millions placed their hope in bulging bank accounts, only to eat the ashes of disillusionment when these bank accounts disappeared in the crash of 1929. During the thirties men placed their hope in their own cleverness and in their own ability to achieve a more abundant life, but the wan faces of agonized millions and the gutted ruins of a continent which boasted of its culture and accomplishments bear silent testimony to the *misplaced* hopes of a generation which was tragically misled.

Only in Christ is there hope, because only in Christ can men find the solution of their deepest needs. It is remarkable how the Bible identifies the entire Christian hope with the person and work of Christ. The Apostle Paul, for instance, after he had told the Christians at Rome all about the forgiveness which was theirs through faith in Jesus Christ, continues by saying: "Therefore, being justified by faith, we have peace with God through our Lord Jesus Christ, by whom also we have access by faith into this grace wherein we stand and *rejoice in hope* of the glory of God. And not only so, but we glory in tribulations also, knowing that tribulation worketh patience; and patience, experience; and experience, *hope.* And hope maketh not ashamed, because the love of God is shed abroad in our

hearts by the Holy Ghost, which is given
unto us." All of Paul's hope for the future
was wrapped up in what he had found in
Christ. He had found forgiveness and peace
in Christ, and he had been assured that this
forgiveness and peace had been given to him
as his priceless and permanent possession.
With these in his heart *to stay*, he had found
a sure foundation for his hope.

> *My hope is built on nothing less*
> *Than Jesus' blood and righteousness;*
> *I dare not trust the sweetest frame,*
> *But wholly lean on Jesus' name.*
> *On Christ, the solid Rock, I stand;*
> *All other ground is sinking sand.*

It is noteworthy how often the New Testament speaks of the hope of the Christian:
"the hope of the Gospel," "the hope of the
promise," "the hope of his calling," "the hope
which is laid up for you in heaven," "our
hope of glory," "hope in our Lord Jesus
Christ," "that blessed hope," "the hope of
eternal life," "the full assurance of hope," "the

hope we have as an anchor," "a lively hope," and scores of other passages. And when the New Testament writers use the word *hope* in connection with the future of the child of God, they use it not in the sense of a pious wish, but in the sense of a sure confidence. The Christian's hope, since it is rooted in the person and promises of Jesus Christ, is a "hope that maketh not ashamed," a hope that is as sure as Christ Himself is sure.

But what does this mean to me? It means that inasmuch as I am a child of God through faith in Jesus Christ, the future holds more good for me than I could ever hope for. Christ is my Guarantee of a blessed future. If God saw fit to send His only Son into the world to suffer and to die that I might live, and if in His mercy He has brought me to faith in Jesus as my Savior, the worst that could ever happen to me is *past*, and the best that can ever happen to me still lies in the future. This is what Scripture means when it says: "He that spared not His own Son, but delivered Him up for us all, how shall

He not with Him also freely give us all
things?" It was this hope of which Paul spoke
when he wrote to his young pupil Titus:
"According to His mercy He saved us . . .
that, being justified by His grace, we should
be made heirs according to the hope of eternal
life." As a child of God, through Christ, I am
an heir of heaven. Eternal life, an unspeakably better life than that which I now am
living, is my heritage. And I can live in the
daily prospect of that better life!

All this is what I mean when I say that
Jesus is my *Hope.* His presence will brighten
every foot of the path that stretches out before me. His promise will uphold me, no
matter what may still confront me. His power
will be my stay in every evil hour. The assurance that I am His and He is mine is my
pledge of eternal life with Him in glory. What
a blessed prospect! What a blessed hope!

> *To Thee, O dear, dear Savior,*
> *My spirit turns to rest.*
> *My peace is in Thy favor,*
> *My pillow on Thy breast;*

Though all the world deceive me,
  I know that I am Thine;
And Thou wilt never leave me,
  O blessed Savior mine.

In Thee my trust abideth,
  On Thee my hope relies,
O Thou whose love provideth
  For all below the skies;
O Thou whose mercy found me,
  From bondage set me free,
And then forever bound me
  With cords of love to Thee.

Oh, for that choicest blessing
  Of living in Thy love
And thus on earth possessing
  The peace of heaven above!
Oh, for the bliss that by it
  The soul securely knows
The holy calm and quiet
  Of faith's serene repose!

Truth

ONE of the deepest cravings of the human heart is to know the truth. The anxious mother's heart would give anything to know the truth about her wayward boy. The lover is hungry for the truth of his beloved. The worried family tosses restlessly on sleepless pillows because it does not know the truth about a father, son, or brother who has been reported missing from the field of battle. — If only they knew *the truth,* there would be an end to this agony of uncertainty.

But a far deeper hunger for the truth is gnawing at the heart of every man and woman. Even the person who professes to have no religion at all will confess in his honest moments that he is troubled by a torturing uncertainty. In the presence of others he may boast that he can get along without a faith in God. He may even proudly assert that there is no God. In his secret heart of hearts, however, he cannot down the haunting question: *But what if there is a God?*

If there is a God, what kind of God is He? What does He think of me? What does He intend to do with me? How do I fit into His plans for the universe, particularly His plans for the human family? What is my personal relationship to Him — and His to me?

Whether a man lives in Chicago, Cleveland, or New York, in Bombay, Calcutta, or Shanghai, he is distressingly conscious of a hunger for the truth about these questions.

And what about a life beyond the grave? Will there be a resurrection? If so, what is to become of me? Will my destiny in the life to come be determined by what I do today? Am I at this moment forging the shackles which will imprison my soul and body in all eternity? Is there a hell? If so, how can I escape it? Is there a heaven? If so, how can I be assured that someday I shall be there? These are questions which have troubled the heart of man down through the ages. And they demand nothing less than *the truth* as their reply.

Furthermore, how am I to get rhyme or reason out of the life I now am living? I eat, I work, I sleep, I awake — I repeat the same process day after day and year after year. But why? For what purpose? Just to wear out and be discarded as a suit of old clothes? Just to move on and make room for others? How am I to fit all the puzzling pieces of my life into a sensible and purposeful pattern — my unemployment, my hospital bills, my bitter disappointments, my failures, my heartaches? Why must these things be? Is there an intelligent plan that lies behind them all and that can give them meaning? I want to know the truth.

I know that men have given answers to all these questions. Philosophers have crowded our libraries with learned books on just these subjects. They have spun impressive theories. But what I need as the polestar of my life — my guide, my chart, my compass — is not a theory that has been invented by a man who is just as subject to error as I am. No, I need the truth — *God's truth.*

I have found that truth — in Jesus!

I have placed my trust in the words of Christ, first of all, because God Himself has told me that the words of Christ are trustworthy. Fifteen hundred years before the birth of Jesus, God spoke to His people through the Prophet Moses and said: "The Lord, thy God, will raise up unto thee a Prophet from the midst of thee . . . unto Him ye shall hearken." Some fifteen hundred years later, after the ascension of the Savior into heaven, Peter addressed an unbelieving multitude and told them that this prophecy had been fulfilled in Jesus. "For Moses truly said unto the fathers: A Prophet shall the Lord, your God, raise up unto you; . . . Him shall ye hear in all things whatsoever He shall say unto you." In other words, God has told me that I am to listen to His Son "in all things whatsoever He shall say unto" me. And so I look to Jesus for the truth.

But more. God the Father placed His stamp of divine approval on His Son and on His teachings both at the occasion of the Savior's

Baptism and again on the Mount of Transfiguration. At the Baptism of our Lord we are told that the Father spoke from heaven, saying: "This is My beloved Son, in whom I am well pleased." On the Mount of Transfiguration, we are told, the Savior's face "did shine as the sun, and His raiment was white as the light," and the Father again spoke from heaven, saying: "This is My beloved Son, in whom I am well pleased; *hear ye Him!*"

Jesus, then, is no mere prophet among many prophets, no mere teacher among many teachers, no mere voice among many voices. He is, by the testimony of God Himself, *the* Teacher. He is the only Voice of God to man. "Hear ye Him!" Surely, a Prophet with those credentials will know the truth. And He will speak the truth. I accept the words of Christ as truth, then, because God Himself has vouched for the truthfulness of His own beloved Son.

I place my trust in the words of Christ, furthermore, because Christ with His own lips has assured me that His Gospel is the truth.

"If ye continue in My Word," He says, "then are ye My disciples indeed; and ye shall know the truth, and the truth shall make you free." To Pilate's question: "Art Thou a king, then?" Jesus replied — knowing that in a matter of hours He would be nailed to a cross — "Thou sayest that I am a king. To this end was I born, and for this cause came I into the world, that I should bear witness to the truth. Everyone that is of the truth heareth My voice."

To the unbelieving people of His day, Jesus said: "I am the Light of the world. He that followeth Me shall not walk in darkness, but shall have the light of life." And shortly before His death He assured His sorrowing disciples: "I am the Way, the *Truth*, and the Life; no man cometh unto the Father but by Me." He not only *knows* the truth, He not only *has* the truth, He not only *brings* the truth: He *is* Truth. He is the Truth of Heaven come down to earth. In Him the stumbling, groping mind of man finds the answer to the deepest problems of the soul.

I place my trust in the words of Christ, finally, because the whole Bible is nothing but one chorus of testimony to the heavenly wisdom of the Savior. To the holy writers, Jesus is God's truth come down from heaven. "In Him are hid all the treasures of wisdom and knowledge," the Bible tells us. "In Him dwelleth all the fullness of the Godhead bodily." John, the disciple whom Jesus loved, opens his Gospel with the well-known words: "In the beginning was the Word [Jesus], and the Word was with God, and the Word was God. . . . And the Word was made flesh and dwelt among us; and we beheld His glory, the glory as of the Only-begotten of the Father, full of grace and truth." To John and to the other Bible writers, Christ was the Word of God, the "Word made flesh," "full of grace and truth."

> *O Word of God Incarnate,*
>   *O Wisdom from on high,*
> *O Truth unchanged, unchanging,*
>   *O Light of our dark sky —*

In a day such as ours, when "darkness covers the earth and gross darkness the people," when men's hearts are failing them for fear, when the hope of ever coming to the knowledge of the truth in spiritual matters is gradually being given up as vain and futile — Christ is still mankind's only hope. He is still the Light of the world. He is still the Way. He is still the Truth.

There are millions on this earth whose problems have been solved in the light of the Gospel of Christ. To them He has become the heavenly Counselor of whom Isaiah prophesied when he looked forward seven hundred years to that first Christmas night and exclaimed: "Unto us a Child is born, unto us a Son is given . . . and His name shall be called Wonderful, *Counselor,* the Mighty God, the Everlasting Father, the Prince of Peace."

Christ has been my Counselor. In Him my life has been given meaning. In Him I have found the answers to those problems of the soul that cry out in the night for an answer. In Him I have found the truth: the truth about

God, the truth about man, the truth about life, the truth about death, the truth about heaven, the truth about hell.

From Him and the sacred pages of His Word I have learned the truth about the origin and destiny of man. I have learned that man is a creature, richly endowed and gifted by God, but ruined because of voluntary sin. I have learned that man, as far as his natural abilities are concerned, is utterly corrupt, completely helpless, and — if left to himself — doomed to an eternal separation from his Maker.

But I have also learned from Christ that God in His mercy has intervened in my behalf. He has sent His only Son into the world to pay the penalty of mankind's guilt, to effect a reconciliation between the Father and His wayward children, and to win a complete redemption for every member of the human family. To achieve this indescribable salvation, Jesus was born, suffered, died, and rose again.

From Christ I have also learned the meaning and purpose of life. I am no longer baffled by its evils, its disappointments, and its heartaches. While there are still many pieces which I am not yet able to fit into the pattern, He has shown me the completed picture and has assured me that every piece has its allotted place in the pattern He has planned. By His suffering and death for my redemption He has given me an overwhelming demonstration of His and His Father's love for me. Assured of *that* love, I can rest assured of His continued guidance and protection. "We know that all things work together for good to them that love God, to them who are the called according to His purpose." "He that spared not His own Son, but delivered Him up for us all, how shall He not with Him also freely give us all things?" These are truths which He has given me. These are truths I trust; and knowing these, I am content.

From Christ I have learned that for me there lies at the end of the road a happy Father's house. "In My Father's house," He assures me, "are many mansions. . . . I go to prepare a place for you. . . . I will come again and receive you unto Myself, that where I am, there ye may be also. And whither I go ye know, and the *way* ye know. . . . I am the Way, the Truth, and the Life; no man cometh unto the Father but by Me." Since I know what lies at the end of the road, the heat of the journey which lies between will not discourage or dismay me.

These are the truths which have been given me, not by any man, but by God Himself. They have been given me by Him of whom the Father said: "This is My beloved Son. . . . Hear ye Him!" I have heard them from the lips of Him who said: "If ye continue in My Word . . . ye shall know the truth." I have been assured of these things by Him whom the Scriptures call "the Word of God," "the Word made flesh." I have been taught these things by Him of whom the Bible says: "In Him are hid all the treasures of wisdom and knowledge." I have been told these things by Him who says: *"I am the Truth!"*

And so, if you ask what Jesus means to me, I answer: To me Jesus is the Truth, Heaven's eternal Truth, God's Truth to man, the only Truth by which a man can set his course and be assured of an eternal destiny of bliss and glory!

Thou art the Way, to Thee alone
  From sin and death we flee;
And he who would the Father seek
  Must seek Him, Lord, by Thee.

Thou art the Truth; Thy Word alone
  True wisdom can impart;
Thou only canst inform the mind
  And purify the heart.

Thou art the Life; the rending tomb
  Proclaims Thy conqu'ring arm;
And those who put their trust in Thee
  Nor death nor hell shall harm.

Thou art the Way, the Truth, the Life;
  Grant us that Way to know,
That Truth to keep, that Life to win,
  Whose joys eternal flow.

Assurance

I n the early days of our country a weary traveler came to the banks of the Mississippi for the first time. There was no bridge by which he could cross. It was early winter, and the surface of the mighty stream was covered with ice. Could he *dare* cross over? Would the uncertain ice be able to bear his weight?

Night was falling, and it was urgent that he reach the other side. Finally, after much hesitation and with many fears, he began to creep cautiously across the surface of the ice on his hands and knees. He thought that thus he might distribute his weight as much as possible and keep the ice from breaking under his heavy load.

About halfway over, he heard the sound of singing behind him. Out of the dusk there came a colored man, driving a four-horse load of coal across the ice and singing merrily as he went his carefree way!

Here was the first man — on his knees, trembling lest the ice be not strong enough to bear him up! And there, as if whisked away by the winter's wind, went the colored man, his horses, his sleigh, and his load of coal — upheld by the same ice on which the first man was creeping! The colored man had gone that way before, he had tested the ice, and he knew that it was well able to carry him and his load safely to the other side.

I have tested Christ. In every scene of life — in joy and sorrow, in success and failure, in health and sickness, in moments of crisis "when every earthly prop gave way" — I have trusted Christ and have found that He was able to carry both me and my burden and bring me safely to the other side. With Paul and with believers of all ages I can say: "I *know* whom I have believed and am *persuaded* that He is able to keep that which I have committed unto Him against that Day." I know the ice won't break!

And this assurance is no mere whistling in the dark, no mere pleasant journey in the land of make-believe. It is firmly rooted in the unshakable promises of an unshakable Book, in the sacred pledge of the world's most sacred Person, and in the experience of millions who can attest to His faithfulness in carrying out His pledge.

But what are the assurances which the Bible gives to those who have come to God through Christ? One of the most beautiful as well as one of the most meaningful Bible assurances is the memorable word of Moses: "The eternal God is thy Refuge, and *underneath are the everlasting arms.*" The story is told of a mother eagle that built her nest on a ledge of rock which jutted precariously over a tremendous precipice. Soaring through the air one day on her return to her nest, she was startled at the sight of her baby eagle struggling on the jagged edge of the rock trying to prevent a fall which was sure to crush its body at the bottom of the canyon. Unable to get to the ledge before her little one would fall, the mother eagle with the speed of lightning swooped low beneath the jutting rock, spread her strong wings to break the fall of her darling, and with her precious cargo clinging to the feathers of her mighty wing, glided safely to the canyon's floor. "The eternal God is thy Refuge, and underneath are the everlasting arms."

Those who have come to God through faith in Christ have found again and again that no matter how acute the danger, no matter how severe the crisis, or how piercing the pain — "underneath are the everlasting arms."

This assurance of the love of God through Christ — a love that not only pardons our sins and thus gives us peace and hope, but a love that goes with us in our daily lives and surrounds us with protecting walls of divine assurance — this is all beyond the understanding of the man who has not yet given his heart into the Savior's keeping. As well talk to a blind man about the colors of the rainbow, or to a deaf man about the song of the nightingale, as try to explain the assurance of the Christian to a man who has not come to faith in Christ. This divine assurance is included in the revelation of which the Bible says: "Eye hath not seen, nor ear heard, neither have entered into the heart of man, the things which God hath prepared for them that love Him."

Nor voice can sing, nor heart can frame,
　　Nor can the mem'ry find,
A sweeter sound than Thy blest name,
　　O Savior of mankind!

O Hope of every contrite heart,
　　O Joy of all the meek!
To those who fall, how kind Thou art,
　　How good to those who seek!

But what to those who find? Ah, this
　　Nor tongue nor pen can show;
The love of Jesus, what it is,
　　None but His loved ones know.

A well-known life insurance company carries a picture of the Rock of Gibraltar on all of its advertising. The rock is the symbol of dependability. It suggests *assurance.* Wind and wave may wreak their havoc, time and

tide may come and go, but the rock endures.
Christ is the Christian's Rock. Millions have
fled to that Rock for refuge and assurance in
the familiar words of Toplady's immortal
hymn:

> *Rock of Ages, cleft for me,*
> *Let me hide myself in Thee!*

Perhaps few people know better what it
means to stand within the shelter of a rock
than those who defended the island of Malta
against the incessant German air bombard-
ments in 1941. From the safe ledges of their
rock-built caverns they watched day after
day — *unharmed* — as chaos and confusion
swirled about them. Outside the rock sure
death would have been theirs. Inside the
rock no danger could befall them.

The rock to which the Christian flees when
all the world seems to be caving in around
him is the shelter of God's assurance, the assurance which God has given him in Christ.
"Fear thou not, for I am with thee. Be not
dismayed, for I am thy God. I will strengthen

thee; yea, I will help thee; yea, I will uphold thee with the right hand of My righteousness." — "Fear not, for I have redeemed thee. I have called thee by thy name; thou art Mine."

These and a thousand other assurances of God were clothed in a human personality when "the Word was made flesh and dwelt among us." Jesus Christ is the personification of all God's assurances. He is the *Rock* of assurance, the *Rock* of salvation, in whom all mankind can find safety and security. Whatever God has offered to men in the way of spiritual assurance, He has offered to them through Christ. "I am the Door," says Jesus, "by Me if any man enter in, he shall be saved and shall go in and out and find pasture."

I have found that pasture. Day after day my heart can feed on the assurances which Christ Himself has given me. He has assured me of His love, His care, His presence, His protection. These are the assurances on which I walk. These are the assurances by which I live. These are the assurances which someday will give strength to my wavering feet when I am called upon to make that final, fateful journey through the valley of death.

Blessed assurance, Jesus is mine!
Oh, what a foretaste of glory divine!
Heir of salvation, purchase of God,
Born of His Spirit, washed in His blood!

Joy

A BRITISH naval officer tells the story of a wealthy native of India who paid a tremendous price to become a Christian. "No sooner had he been baptized," writes the officer, "than all of his possessions were taken from him, and his wife and children disowned him." One day the officer asked the former rich man: "Are you able to bear your troubles?" The poor man replied: "Many people ask me that, but they never ask me whether I am able to bear my *joys;* for I enjoy a happiness in my heart since I know Christ which no one has been able to take from me."

The spiritual experience of this man has been the experience of every man, woman, and child who has ever put his faith in Jesus Christ as his personal Savior. I, too, have had the same experience. Of all the joys of life, I have found none greater, none more exciting, than the sure knowledge that, through Christ, God has become my Father, my sins have been washed away, and heaven is my assured possession.

The religion of Jesus Christ is essentially a religion of joy. It is a caricature of the truth to picture the Christian as a man with a long face, a heavy book, and a black umbrella. The life of Christ itself is a living contradiction of the claim that to be a consistent Christian one must be an apostle of gloom. The Savior mingled freely with the common people of His day, took part in their innocent pleasures, and hallowed their homely joys with the benediction of His presence. The Pharisees of His day frequently complained that Jesus was not as strict as John the Baptist, that He mingled too freely with common folks, and that His whole demeanor was lacking in the austerity and severity which they had become accustomed to associate with a prophet. "This man receiveth sinners and eateth with them," they murmured.

Christ had come to earth to proclaim a religion of joy. Already on the night of His birth the angel messenger had announced: "Fear not, for, behold, I bring you good tidings of great *joy,* which shall be to all people. For unto you is born this day in the city of David a Savior, which is Christ the Lord." Wherever He went, throughout His earthly life, He brought joy to the sorrowing, cheer to the downcast, and gladness to those who were sitting in the shadow of death. The supreme aim of His earthly ministry was to restore joy to human hearts which had been languishing in the shackles of sin and sadness.

It is significant how frequently the Savior referred to this joy on the night before His crucifixion. After speaking to His disciples at length concerning their intimate relationship with Him, which would continue even after His death and resurrection—using the familiar symbol of the Vine and the branches — He says to them: "These things have I spoken unto you that My joy might remain in you and that your joy might be full." His continued presence in their lives was to be a continuing source of joy and gladness — also after they could no longer see Him. But as the Savior peered into the future that night, He could see the inevitable trials which would beset the lives of those who put their trust in Him, and so He assures His believers: "Ye shall be sorrowful, but your sorrow shall be turned into joy . . . and your joy no man taketh from you." Your joy will be your permanent possession.

Anyone who takes the time to read the history of the early Christian Church as it is given in the books of the New Testament will agree that *joy* was the dominant note of the lives of Christ's Apostles. This does not mean that the lives of Christ's followers were cushioned by beds of roses. No, there were hardships to be endured. But they found joy in the midst of hardship, gladness in the midst of pain. "As sorrowful, yet always rejoicing; as poor, yet making many rich" is the way the Bible puts it.

Thus, for instance, after Peter and his companions had been beaten and thrown into prison for having preached the Gospel, we read that "they departed from the presence of the Council, *rejoicing* that they were counted worthy to suffer shame for His name." And later on we are told that after Paul and Silas had been cruelly beaten and thrown into the inner dungeon, "at midnight Paul and Silas prayed and sang praises unto God." They had experienced a joy that was so deep, so firm, so sure that the trials of life were but as the ripples on the surface of the sea. Their joy was undisturbed. "Your joy no man taketh from you."

And they were eager that others become partakers of their joy. Again and again we hear them offering the joy of the Gospel, the joy of salvation, to others. "Rejoice in the Lord alway, and again I say, Rejoice!" St. Paul writes to his Philippians. "Rejoice evermore!" is his exhortation to the Thessalonians. Enumerating the blessings of the Christian faith, Paul writes to the Galatians: "But the fruit of the spirit is love, *joy*, peace. . . ." To the Romans he writes: "The kingdom of God is . . . righteousness and peace and *joy* in the Holy

Ghost." And Peter writes to the Christians
who had been scattered throughout Asia
Minor that since they have come to a knowledge of salvation through faith in the blood
of their Redeemer, they now "rejoice with joy
unspeakable and full of glory." To Christ, to
His Apostles, and to the early Christians the
message of the Gospel was a message of joy —
and the life of the believer was a life of gladness based upon that message.

> *Oh, for a thousand tongues to sing*
> *My great Redeemer's praise,*
> *The glories of my God and King,*
> *The triumphs of His grace!*

> *Jesus! — the name that charms our fears,*
> *That bids our sorrows cease;*
> *'Tis music in the sinner's ears,*
> *'Tis life and health and peace.*

The joy of the Christian, says the Bible, is
a joy "in the Lord." It finds its reason in
Christ. The permanence of our joy usually
depends upon the reason for our joy. The joy
of the child who has just been given an ice-

cream cone will be short-lived because of the passing nature of the object of its joy. The joy of the young man who finds supreme satisfaction in the exercise of his youthful vigor will begin to fade as youth gives way to old age. The joy of the young lady who has found her highest good in her charm and beauty will last no longer than these attractions. And the joy of the businessman who has attached his heart to wealth and influence will crumble into dust on the day that his possessions are taken from him. Yes, it is true, the permanence of our joy depends upon the reason for our joy. That is why the Christian's joy is always "in the Lord."

Some time ago I came across these remarkable paragraphs. In answer to the question *Where Is Happiness?* the anonymous author answers:

Not in Unbelief —

Voltaire was an infidel of the most pronounced type. He wrote: "I wish I had never been born."

Not in Pleasure —

Lord Byron lived a life of pleasure, if anyone did. He wrote: "The worm, the canker, and the grief are mine alone."

Not in Money —

Jay Gould, the American millionaire, had plenty of that. When dying, he said: "I suppose I am the most miserable man on earth."

Not in Position and Fame —

Lord Beaconsfield enjoyed more than his share of both. He wrote: "Youth is a mistake; manhood, a struggle; old age, a regret."

Not in Military Glory —

Alexander the Great conquered the known world in his day. Having done so, he wept in his tent, because, he said, "There are no more worlds to conquer."

Where, Then, Is Happiness Found?

The answer is simple: In Christ alone. He said: "I will see you again, and your heart shall rejoice, and your joy no man taketh from you."

What Jesus was to His disciples and to the believers of the early church He is still to millions of believing souls throughout the world today. The Christian is the happiest man in all the world. In fact, no one in all the world has a better right to joy and gladness than the trusting child of God. He alone knows beyond the shadow of a doubt that all his sins have been forgiven and that through Christ he has a clear title to a mansion in the Father's house above. He alone has the divine assurance of comfort in sorrow, strength in sickness, solace in bereavement, help in distress, and ultimate triumph in the midst of dire calamity. And this assurance is signed and sealed in the blood of the Son of God Himself. The world has known no higher guarantee.

This joy, the unspeakable joy of the child of God, is mine. I have found that, no matter what the circumstance, no matter how fraught with gloom the prospect, no matter how discouraging or disconcerting the difficulty — I could nevertheless tap that reservoir of joy which God has placed into every human heart that has come to Him through Christ. The assurance of His pardon, His peace, His power, His presence in every scene of life, has emptied my life of gloom and sadness and filled it with a high and holy gladness. It was this deep and all-pervading assurance which moved the learned Horatius Bonar to exclaim:

> *All that I was, my sin, my guilt,*
> *My death, was all mine own;*
> *All that I am, I owe to Thee,*
> *My gracious God, alone.*

> *The evil of my former state*
> *Was mine, and only mine;*
> *The good in which I now rejoice*
> *Is Thine, and only Thine.*

The darkness of my former state,
* The bondage, all was mine;*
The light of life in which I walk,
* The liberty, is Thine.*

Thy Word first made me feel my sin,
* It taught me to believe;*
Then, in believing, peace I found,
* And now I* LIVE! *I* LIVE!

What does Jesus mean to me? He means joy, joy unspeakable, joy already here on earth and eternally in heaven!

Heaven

A LITTLE girl was walking with her father along a country road. The night was clear, and the child was enthralled by the splendor of the sky, all lit up with twinkling stars from one end to the other. After moments of reflection she suddenly looked up to her father and said: "Daddy, I was just thinking — if the *wrong* side of heaven is so beautiful, how wonderful the *right* side must be!"

No tongue or pen has ever succeeded in describing the glory, the grandeur, and the magnificence of the Father's house above. That it is a place of entrancing beauty and matchless splendor the Apostle John indicates in the Book of Revelation by describing heaven's glories in terms of costly jewels and precious gems and rarest metals.

How could heaven be anything else but beautiful! It is the habitation of our God, the royal palace of the King of kings! And in that palace — oh, wondrous thought! — the

Son of God has gone to prepare a place for those who trust Him as their Savior. Through faith in His redeeming mercy they will ascend someday to His home beyond the skies — more exquisite, more glorious, more wonderful, than human speech can tell!

> *Jerusalem the golden,*
> *With milk and honey blest!*
> *Beneath thy contemplation*
> *Sink heart and voice oppressed;*
> *I know not, oh, I know not*
> *What joys await us there,*
> *What radiancy of glory,*
> *What bliss beyond compare!*

Yes, I know not what joys await me there; but I do know, as sure as God's own Word is true, that heaven's glories shall be mine. And I have found this immovable assurance in Jesus Christ, my Savior. One of the most tender chapters in the entire Bible is that passage which describes the solemn meeting of the Savior with His faithful few on the night in which He was betrayed. There, in the very shadow of approaching death, Jesus comforted His despondent followers with the memorable words: "Let not your heart be troubled. . . . In My Father's house are many mansions; if it were not so, I would have told you. I go to prepare a place for you. And if I go and prepare a place for you, I will come again and receive you unto Myself; that where I am, there ye may be also." — Those words of Jesus Christ, my Savior, mean more to me than all the gold and silver of a thousand hills!

There is something about the life beyond the grave that fills our hearts with dreadful awe and solemn wonder. Even the thought of heaven — with its unspeakable glory and grandeur — sometimes frightens us, and we ask: "Will I feel at home in heaven? Will I be at ease in the celestial mansions?" How wonderfully all our fears, all our misgivings, are silenced when, with the Savior, we can point to heaven and say: "My *Father's* house!" Through Christ, the Ruler of the rolling spheres has become my Father, and going to heaven is a happy homecoming, a blessed

reunion of the Father with His children. What
comfort, what strength, what joy are mine —
in the knowledge that beyond the portals of
eternity there lies a friendly Father's house!

As the Savior that night looked out across
the centuries and saw all the countless throngs
who would be brought to faith in Him, He
thought it fitting to remind them that the
expanse of His Father's house is limitless —
there will be room enough for all who come
to the Father through faith in Him. And so
He assures His followers: "In My Father's
house are *many* mansions."

I may be sure: there is room enough for
me! He whose love singled me out as an
object of His all-redeeming mercy and who
has promised to preserve me unto the day of
His heavenly kingdom — He has prepared and
reserved a room for me. He has claimed and
is holding my place in the eternal mansions.
"I know whom I have believed and am persuaded that He is able to keep that which
I have committed unto Him against that Day,"
says the Apostle Paul. "Henceforth there is

laid up for me a crown of righteousness which the Lord, the righteous Judge, shall give me at that Day; and not to me only, but unto all them also that love His appearing."

There is something significant about every reference of the Savior to His Father's house. He speaks as one who had been there! "If it were not so, I would have told you!" As one who stands on a mountaintop looking down into the valley beyond and telling his comrades behind him what he sees, so the Savior tells us about His Father's house and ours. The streets of the eternal city are familiar to Him. The mansions of the Father's house stand clear and bright before His vision. He *knows* what lies beyond the valley, because He has come from there. That is why He could speak of heaven and say: "If it were not so, I would have told you." What a strengthening assurance to have as one's dearest Friend Him who has already spent endless ages in the eternal Father's house, who knows the way, and who by His innocent suffering and death for our sins upon the cross has opened up that way for us! Into the hands of such a divine Redeemer we can surely entrust our souls for time and for eternity.

There was another tender note of reassurance in the words which Christ spoke to His faithful few that night, a note which has poured faith and courage into the hearts of Christian people ever since. "I will come again!" — As a mother soothes her weeping child, from whom she must be parted for a moment, with the whisper of assurance, "I will come again," so the Savior seeks to soothe the fears of His disciples with the comforting assurance of His imminent return. I must leave you now, He says, but — "let not your heart be troubled . . . I will come again."

And how effectively that simple promise of the Savior instilled fresh courage into their fainting hearts throughout the coming years is seen from Bible history. Trials and afflictions, pains and persecutions — all would have to be borne, to be sure — but only until He would come again. Then all would be supremely well. His coming, either at the death of the

world or at the death of His disciples, cast
a golden glow over all the road that lay ahead.
They were walking toward the light of His
return. And in that light all shadows fell
behind them.

So, too, in the lives of all who have put
their trust in the might and mercy of the
Savior. All sorrows, all heartaches, all disappointments and bereavements, lose their
bitterness in the sweetness of the Savior's
tender promise: "I will come again." I will
come again to turn your sorrows into joy,
your heartaches into gladness, your bereavements into heavenly reunions in My Father's
house above.

It was that same night that Jesus prayed to
His Father and said: "Father, I will that they
also whom Thou hast given Me be with Me
where I am, that they may behold My glory,
which Thou hast given Me; for Thou lovedst
Me before the foundation of the world." He
shares with His Father a desire which, when
He repeats it to His disciples, becomes
a promise: "I will come again and receive you

unto Myself, that *where I am there ye may be also."* Jesus has secured His Father's approval and permission to bring His friends with Him to share His glory in the Father's house. By His suffering, death, and resurrection He has unlocked the door of His Father's home — and heaven has become an open house! That is why He could say: "Where I am, there ye" — ye who have come to the Father by Me — "may be also."

> *"Forever with the Lord!"*
> *Amen! So let it be.*
> *Life from the dead is in that word,*
>   *'Tis immortality!*

But can I be sure that Christ has the power to fulfill these promises? Yes, I can be sure! Why? Because Christ Himself has risen from the dead and proved Himself the Victor over sin and death and hell. More than sixty years after His death and resurrection and ascension into heaven He appeared to His beloved Apostle John (the man who recorded the comforting words of the Savior about the mansions of His Father's house) and said to him: "I am He that liveth and was dead; and behold, I am alive forevermore and have the keys of hell and of death." By His resurrection from the dead Christ proved Himself the Son of God with power to keep His promises. His victory over the grave is our pledge of life eternal. His empty tomb proclaims to us that someday our grave, too, shall be empty. "Because I live, ye shall live also," He assures every one of His believers. "I am the Resurrection and the Life; he that believeth in Me, though he were dead, yet shall he live; and whosoever liveth and believeth in Me shall never die." It was because of Christ's resurrection that the Apostle could exclaim: "O Death, where is thy sting? O Grave, where is thy victory? The sting of death is sin, and the strength of sin is the Law. But thanks be to God, which giveth us the victory through our Lord Jesus Christ." And the same Apostle says in another passage: "But now is Christ risen from the dead and become the First Fruits of them that slept." Just as the first fruits are the forepledge, the foretaste, of the later and more general harvest, so Christ's resurrection is the guarantee and forepledge of *our* resurrection to life immortal — in that later, greater harvest. Christ's resurrection is God's final stamp of approval on the redeeming work of His Son. And now — because He lives, we, too, shall live.

I know that my Redeemer lives;
What comfort this sweet sentence gives!
He lives, He lives, who once was dead;
He lives, my everliving Head.

He lives to bless me with His love,
He lives to plead for me above,
He lives my hungry soul to feed,
He lives to help in time of need.

He lives and grants me daily breath;
He lives, and I shall conquer death;
He lives my mansion to prepare;
He lives to bring me safely there.

Yes, "He lives to bring me safely there." In that distant home lies the complete fulfillment of all my highest hopes. There dwells my

Savior, who has prepared my mansion for me — and has prepared me for my mansion. There dwell those whom "I love most and best." And there — blessed thought! — I, too, someday shall dwell!

And I shall dwell there solely because of the unmerited goodness and grace of God, whose gift to all believers "is eternal life through Jesus Christ, our Lord." Small wonder that the greatest Apostle of them all, as he contemplated the vexations and the vanities of this present world, could say during the closing years of his life: "I have a desire to depart and to be with Christ, which is far better." And again: "For me to live is Christ, and to die is gain."

What does Jesus mean to me?

> *Chief of sinners though I be,*
> *Christ is All in all to me;*
> *Died that I might live on high;*
> *Lived that I might never die;*
> *As the branch is to the vine,*
> *I am His, and He is mine!*

Index to Bible Passages

A list of all Bible passages quoted in this book, arranged according to the sequence in which they appear on each page

Index to Bible Passages